Extraordinary Information That
Will Revolutionize Your Life

NO ONE
TOLD ME

VERN FRANK II

No One Told Me

Vern Frank II

No One Told Me
ISBN: 978-1-7354232-1-0
Copyright © 2020 by Vern Frank II

Table Of Contents

Chapter One
I NEED TO TELL
YOU SOMETHING

I am writing this book to share with you something that changed my life. Throughout life there are things we learn which can help us tremendously as we live our lives. Learning 2+2=4 is a very important piece of knowledge that changes our lives. Learning how to drive is yet another event that changes our lives, and learning how to read is one of the biggest things we can do to change our lives for the better in this world.

Many times, there are things we do not know that can change our lives. Just yesterday I read something no dentist has ever told me. After brushing my teeth, I am not supposed to rinse out my mouth. The article said that rinsing (which I always have done) does not allow the fluoride to sit on my teeth and work. It was shocking to find this out so late in my life! Immediately, I changed my brushing habits. This change could allow me to keep all my teeth for the rest of my life.

What if I had some insider information about life and I decided to keep it to myself instead of sharing it with you? What if I kept information to myself which could change your life forever? This would be very selfish of me. In fact, it could be considered hateful. To withhold information I have found which could benefit you now and forever would not be doing the right thing as a human being.

At the age of 19, I found out no one had told me the most significant piece of information that any human can know. This information changed everything in my life. It changed me from the inside out--forever. This information is the most important thing that can ever be shared with anyone.

Now, before I go any further, please throw out any preconceived notions of what you think I am going to say. Please throw out any prejudices you might have. This information will lead you to the best event to ever happen in your life. This is not a joke! It is serious and it is going to be a life changer for you if you will receive the words I am going to say next.

The biggest piece of knowledge any human can acquire or learn in this life is that you must call Jesus your Lord and Savior if you are going to receive eternal life and live forever with Him.

Now, your first thought might be, "I don't need religion," or "I go to church," or even, "I was baptized as a baby." Please get rid of those thoughts right now. Those thoughts are going to cause you to miss the best party that will ever take place. At the end of time, there is going to be a party in heaven like no one has ever seen. I want to be at that party with you.

The truth many people miss, even people who go to church and are "religious", is that Jesus must be confessed as Lord by every person individually. Going to church is not the thing that changes you. Being baptized as a baby or as an adult is not the thing that changes you. Even reading the Bible does not change you unless you receive the words of the Bible as truth and you let them change you. Each person must call on the name of the Lord Jesus if they are going to have a relationship with God.

You might be saying, "Why is this necessary?" In order to understand we need to go back to the beginning.

Chapter Two
WHY IS THIS NECESSARY?

The reason each person must call Jesus their Lord is because each person already has a lord by default. The lord I am talking about is Satan. Satan is actually an angel who tried to make himself higher than God and was kicked out of heaven. He was once called Lucifer (light-bringer) because he was a bearer of light. He was one of the most beautiful creations of God. You might be thinking, "I don't believe in Satan" but when we realize that Satan is real it will help us understand why the earth is filled with so much evil.

The first man, Adam, bowed his knee to Satan and obeyed his voice rather than the voice of God. Since that time man has been under the rule of Satan and sin has ruled in the earth. This is why there is so much chaos and destruction on the earth. This is why there is so much pain and suffering on the earth.

Many people think God is in control of everything. That is not true! God gave man authority to rule on the earth at the beginning of time, but man handed his authority over to Satan. Satan became the god of this world we live in when Adam disobeyed God and instead chose to obey Satan.

These things are not talked about much anymore and they may sound fictional, but there are real spiritual forces all around us. There is a spiritual world we don't see. There are demonic forces, angels, a Holy Spirit, and a Kingdom of Heaven. There are many spiritual things that are not seen. The Bible says everything that is seen is temporary, but everything not seen is eternal.

One of those eternal things we don't see is our soul. Every person has a soul. This soul is where we make our decisions. It is where God gave each person a free will. Free will is the ability to choose the path you want to take. You might remember seeing an illustration of a devil sitting on one shoulder of a person and an angel sitting on the other shoulder. One being is trying to get the person to do wrong and the other being is trying to get the person to do good. This is truer than we think. There are spiritual forces trying daily to get people to join their side and choices are made regarding who to follow.

Jesus came into this world to get mankind back on the side of God. He came into this world to rescue mankind from the lordship of Satan. God became flesh to bring mankind back into His family. Jesus is called the second Adam because He has won back the authority for mankind. Because everyone has a soul, every person on earth can now choose Jesus to be their Lord and come out from under the lordship of Satan. This is called salvation. Salvation simply means we are saved from all the punishment we deserved.

God created man as a beautiful being who had perfect fellowship with God. God created mankind to rule on the earth. Mankind was clothed with the glory of God and when they disobeyed God, they realized they were naked for the first time. Mankind disobeyed God and became a fallen being. As a fallen being, man needed someone to bridge the divide that was now between him and God. There had to be someone who could take the punishment that was deserved in order to restore man's fellowship with God. Jesus was that person.

Jesus took all the wrath of God upon Himself and all the punishment we deserved. Jesus is the only answer for every person to be restored back into the family of God. Jesus must be the one we call upon to come back into God's family. We can hope there is another way but there is not. Jesus is the only way.

The reason all of this was done for us is because God loves every person on earth. God's love reached out to this earth through Jesus. His love must be received if we are to be in a relationship with God. If someone loves you deeply but you do not receive their love, you will never enter into a relationship with them.

The same is true in our relationship with God. His love has reached out to us and we must receive that love. We have to receive what God has done for us through Jesus and allow God to enter into our lives. My hope in writing this book is that you receive His love and enter into a relationship with your Creator.

I encourage you to study this further if you have doubts. There are so many answers available if we will only look for them. These are topics that matter for all eternity. Don't just hope these things are not true. Find out for yourself. Your eternal soul is on the line here.

You have time right now to study for yourself. You have a chance right now to choose the Lord Jesus and receive eternal life. You will not have this choice forever. There is a time when all men will be judged and the only correct answer at that time is, "I chose Jesus to be my Lord and Savior and He took all my sin upon Himself so I no longer deserve any punishment."

Through Jesus, mankind has been restored into a relationship with God. As in any relationship there are different benefits available because we are friends with that person. You might be friends with a very wealthy person and receive some benefits from that connection during your life. You might be friends with a very funny person and receive some joyful benefits from knowing them. When we are friends with God there are many benefits which go along with that relationship. Salvation has many parts that will give you everything you need.

Chapter Three
WHAT IS SALVATION?

What is the first thing you think of when I say the word *salvation*? Many people think of it as going to heaven. That is a good thought. That is a true thought. I would say most Christians and even non-Christians think of heaven when thinking of salvation. I want to look at this word more in-depth than just the thought of heaven.

Salvation is a word that can change your entire life right now on this earth. With a correct understanding of salvation, our life on earth can change dramatically and our tomorrow can be much better. When we get a true understanding of salvation it will not only change our future, but it will change our present.

"To be saved from sin" means to be kept safe and sound; rescued and preserved from danger and destruction; the suffering one saved from perishing; delivered from penalties of judgment; made whole in spirit, soul, and body. Wow! This is what Jesus did for us. Jesus, of course, is the Savior. That is what His name means. Jesus means Savior. Jesus came to bring salvation to all. Jesus came to save everyone.

John 3:17
For God did not send His Son into the world to condemn the world, but that the world through Him might be saved.

Jesus came to keep us safe and sound and rescue us from danger. Jesus came to save us from perishing eternally and to deliver us from the penalties of judgment. He came to make us whole in our spirit, soul, and body. That is some good news! This is why the news about Jesus is called the Gospel which means "good news."

We also need to understand that salvation is past, present, and future. First, our spirit has been saved (we were delivered from the penalty of sin). We were spiritually dead because of sin and were not alive unto God. When we confess Jesus as our Lord and Savior, our spirit is born again. Our sins were completely washed away when we were born again. Our spirit was made alive unto God when we were saved.

Secondly, our soul is being saved (we are being delivered from the power of sin). We are to actively pursue sanctification. *Sanctification* is a big word that means *we are set apart for God*. We should not be seeking how we can sin. We should be actively seeking to obey God. We should desire to obey God in every area of our lives.

Thirdly, our body will be saved. We will receive a glorified body when we go to heaven. At that point there will no longer be any presence of sin. On that day, our salvation will be complete. What a wonderful day that will be!

Hopefully, you are starting to see how wonderful Jesus is. You are starting to see how wonderful salvation is. There are many things that happen in us at the moment of salvation and we will cover some of those things in the following chapters.

Chapter Four
WE ARE RECONCILED

2 Corinthians 5:18
Now all things are of God, who has reconciled us to Himself through Jesus Christ, and has given us the ministry of reconciliation.

When a person is saved, they are immediately reconciled to God. Reconciled means friendly relations have been restored. Because of Jesus, a truce has been declared between God and man. God, through Jesus, has said to every person on this planet that He wants to make peace with them.

God had a plan from the beginning of time that would bring man back into a good relationship with Himself. This can be seen in Genesis 3:15: "And I will put enmity between you and the woman, and between your seed and her Seed; He shall bruise your head, and you shall bruise His heel." In this verse, God told the devil that there was someone coming that would destroy his power over mankind. God knew mankind would mess up. God knew we would need a Savior.

He also knew exactly what He was going to do to solve this relationship problem before the first sin ever happened. From the very beginning of time, God planned to send Jesus to destroy the works of the devil.

The wrath of God no longer abides on anyone who has called Jesus their Lord. This change happens immediately when anyone receives what Jesus did for them. It is not something that is going to happen or a promise that is yet to be fulfilled. We do not need to wait for something to happen. Instantly, as soon as someone says, "Jesus is my Lord", God's wrath is gone!

If you are ready to make Jesus your Lord right now and receive eternal life, please pray the following prayer:

Dear God in heaven, I realize I need forgiveness. I realize I need a Savior. I turn away from sin. I believe Jesus died for me. I believe His blood was shed for me. I believe He rose from the dead for me. I now call Jesus my Lord and my Savior so now I am saved according to Your Word. Fill me with Your Holy Spirit. Teach me how to live for You. Thank You for giving me eternal life. Thank You for making me complete. I now call You my Father God forever and ever! In Jesus name I pray. Amen!

If you prayed this prayer from your heart, you have become a born-again Christian. You have made Jesus your Lord. You have entered the family of God. You have received eternal life. You have made the best decision you will ever make.

Now, notice the last part of 2 Corinthians 5:18 above says He has given us the ministry of reconciliation. This is why I am writing this book. Every person who receives Jesus is now called to tell someone else about Jesus. Every person who receives Jesus is in the ministry.

It is not just apostles, pastors, evangelists, and prophets who are supposed to tell someone about Jesus. Everyone who makes Jesus the Lord of their life needs to go and tell more people about the good news.

If you have made Jesus your Lord, then it's time for you to tell someone about Jesus. It's time for you to tell someone that they can be in a relationship with God. Some will not listen to you. Some will listen to you but not really care what you have to say. Some will listen and receive the good news and make Jesus their Lord. Our job is not to make anybody receive the good news. Our job is to tell others the good news.

So, I challenge you to go right now and tell someone about Jesus. Ask them if they want to know God and have a personal relationship with Him. Tell them what you have learned so far about God. You don't have to go to Bible school or be a Christian for five years before telling someone about Jesus.

The best time to tell someone about Jesus is as soon as you get saved because the love of God is burning on the inside of you and that love wants to be let out. That love for people burning on the inside of you is God. God wants you to tell someone else so that another person can be reconciled to Him.

Chapter Five
WE ARE REDEEMED

Colossians 1:14
In whom we have redemption through
His blood, the forgiveness of sins.

To truly understand the word *redemption*, we need to see this word in its cultural context. In the ancient world, men, women, and children were routinely bought and sold. They were purchased, owned, traded, and put to work. These slaves could be handed down from one generation to another. A person might be born into slavery, or they might go into debt and then become slaves to pay their debt. Some were captured by an enemy army and then made slaves in a different country.

In the days of the Bible, there were only two ways a slave could ever be freed. One, a condemned man might have enough money to pay the price and purchase his own freedom. Two, someone took pity upon a slave and they chose to purchase that slave with their money; then, having purchased a slave, they could set the slave free.

The purchase price for a slave was called the "redemption money." So, to *redeem* means to *see a slave, pay the price, take them off the market and then set them free.* One man pays the redemption money so that another man can go free.

The only hope for mankind was for someone to redeem us from slavery to sin. We didn't need a counselor. We didn't need a change of attitude. We didn't even need a change of scenery. We needed a redeemer. The heart of the Gospel is all about redemption.

We were taken off the slave market of sin when we called Jesus our Lord. No longer slaves to sin, we are completely free because the price has been paid in full. Jesus paid the ransom price. Jesus stepped down from heaven and said, "I will pay the price for everyone on the earth."

Imagine how happy a slave would be if they were redeemed and completely free to go do whatever they wanted to do! I am sure there were shouts of joy from the slaves that were set free. If you have already called Jesus your Lord then you have been redeemed. You have been taken from the slave market of sin. That means it is time to rejoice. Right now, lift up your voice and give thanks to God that you have been forever set free!

I read a story awhile back about George Wilson. He was a bank robber who was caught and sentenced to be executed in 1830. Some influential people asked for Wilson to receive a pardon from President Andrew Jackson. President Jackson issued a full pardon for this man. Wilson then refused to accept the pardon. The Supreme Court even ruled that Wilson had to accept the pardon granted to him or he would still be executed. Wilson was offered a full pardon but he would not receive it.

Just as with Wilson, what Jesus did for every person on this planet must be received by each person individually. Without Jesus, every person on earth is condemned to eternal death for sin against God. Without Jesus, every person on earth is a slave to sin. Jesus had pity on us and came into our world. He came into Satan's slave market to redeem all the slaves.

Jesus was willing to pay any price for us. The one man who could redeem us chose to pay the price. The price was His blood. Jesus chose to pay the ransom price in full with His blood. Jesus became a replacement for us. He is our redeemer.

The redemption price has been paid and everyone can receive a full pardon from the punishment they deserve, but they must receive the freedom that has been provided through Jesus.

Chapter Six
WE ARE COMPLETELY FORGIVEN

Colossians 2:13
And you, being dead in your trespasses and the uncircumcision of your flesh, He has made alive together with Him, having forgiven you all trespasses.

One thing holding many people back from doing what God wants them to do in life is the feeling that they have done too many wrong things. Sometimes people look back at their past and they can't get over what they did at one time in their life. They don't feel worthy to serve the Lord or be in the ministry.

A man who might have felt that way was Peter. Peter was very close to Jesus. He even said he would die for Jesus. On the night when Jesus was betrayed by Judas, Peter denied the Lord three times, just like Jesus said he would do. Peter felt horrible and I do not doubt he was thinking about quitting the ministry completely and going back to fishing full-time.

Jesus, after rising from the dead, comes to talk to Peter one-on-one. Jesus knew Peter needed to be restored. As Jesus talked with Peter, Peter realizes that the Lord was not mad at him. In fact, this was when Peter received his assignment from Jesus to "Feed my sheep." A few days later, Peter was preaching powerful sermons and seeing thousands call on the name of Jesus. By this, we can see how Peter received forgiveness and went on to do the will of God with all his might.

Another man who definitely could have felt this way was Saul, who became Paul. Saul was a Jewish religious leader. After Jesus rose from the dead, Saul began persecuting the Christians because he believed they were ruining the true faith. He believed they were heretics and worthy of death. He even held the coats of those who stoned Stephen, an early Christian evangelist, to death. Stephen was telling the people about Jesus and Saul was happy to see him die.

When Saul was saved, he had to put his past behind him. He received the revelation that he was completely forgiven. To move on with God, he knew he had to forget his past mistakes.

He said in Philippians 3:13-14, "Brethren, I

do not count myself to have apprehended; but one thing I do, forgetting those things which are behind and reaching forward to those things which are ahead, I press toward the goal for the prize of the upward call of God in Christ Jesus." Saul even changed his name to Paul. Paul realized in order to keep moving forward in God he had to forget the past.

We must also forget the past because the past sins we committed have been forgiven. Our sins are not partially forgiven in Christ; they are completely forgiven in Christ. The sins that stained our life have been washed away. We have been made white as snow. Psalm 103:12 says, "As far as the east is from the west, so far has He removed our transgressions from us." Micah 7:19 says, "He will again have compassion on us, and will subdue our iniquities. You will cast all our sins into the depths of the sea."

God is not trying to hold our past against us. He did not send Jesus so we could be partially forgiven. Jesus was sent into the world so that mankind could be completely forgiven of every trespass against God. Since we are completely forgiven, we can serve the Lord without any fear of Him. We can know God is not holding any grudges against us for our past mistakes. God desires we let go of the past and move forward to accomplish His will for our lives, just like Peter and Paul.

Chapter Seven
WE ARE FOREVER
IN CHRIST

Romans 6:11
Likewise you also, reckon yourselves to be dead indeed to sin, but alive to God in Christ Jesus our Lord.

One of the greatest truths to understand when we are born again is that we are now found in Christ. We immediately go from out of Christ to in Christ at the moment of salvation. We immediately go from having absolutely nothing good in us to having everything good in Christ. We immediately go from dead in sin to forever alive in Christ. We go from defeated out of Christ to victorious in Christ.

There is no better place to be than in Christ. It is the safest, most peaceful, most beautiful, most joyful, and most loving place to be. It is the only place to be if we want to live forever.

I am always amazed how many people try and find themselves somewhere else rather than in Christ. They want to discover who they are. They go to different countries to try and discover who they are. They try different careers and many different relationships to see if they can find themselves that way. The truth is we will never really find ourselves until we are found in Christ. This is where every person is supposed to be.

Because of sin, mankind was removed from being in God but now, through Christ, every person can come back into God. We were created to always be a part of God's family. We were created to always be in God's presence. Through Jesus the Christ we can all come back where we belong.

There is no other place that compares to being in Christ. We can go to Hawaii and see beautiful things but it does not even compare to being in Christ. We can go to Europe and see amazing historical sites but it does not even come close to being in Christ. Getting a hold of this truth will change our daily walk with our God.

A good study to do is to find all the Bible verses that speak about who we are in Christ. There are many verses that tell us who we have been made in Christ. These verses will absolutely revolutionize our walk with God when we believe what they tell us. For example, the verse above says that we are alive to God in Christ Jesus our Lord. There is so much truth in that we could think on it all day or all year.

We are now alive to God! No longer are we trying to find God or ourselves. We do not have to seek out a book about how to connect to God. We have been found in Christ and we never have to leave that place. We can stay in Christ forever and forever.

We must realize that we are already alive to God in Christ. We can talk to God anytime. We have a direct connection to the One who created us. The phone line is always open. There is never a busy signal. In Christ, we have gone from eternal death to eternal life. We have blessing after blessing to look forward to for all eternity. Just this one truth will change our lives if we ever get a hold of it.

Chapter Eight
WE ARE EMPOWERED
BY GRACE

Romans 6:14
For sin shall not have dominion over you, for you are not under law but under grace.

Because of the grace of God, sin can no longer dominate us unless we allow it to. We no longer have to sin. The grace of God has been given us to overcome every problem in our lives.

The law (The Ten Commandments) showed us the way we should live if we wanted to live a perfect life before our God. The problem was the law could not be completely fulfilled by any human until Jesus came. Because of this the Bible says, "All have sinned and fallen short of the glory of God (Romans 3:23)." The law was not meant to perfect us but to show us that we needed a Savior. When we stop trying to reach perfection in our own strength, then, and only then, are we ready to receive the answer for our shortcomings. Then, and only then, can we call Jesus our Lord and Savior.

Now, in the life of a born-again Christian, the grace of God rules if we will allow it. We must receive the grace of God (Romans 5:17). The grace of God is a gift. When someone gives us a gift for our birthday, we have to receive it. However, we can reject a birthday gift if we choose.

God has given us His gift of grace and that gift is always available. When the grace of God is received it empowers us to overcome every obstacle. The grace of God enables us to do the will of God. The grace of God makes us victorious when it looks like we are going to lose.

One of the greatest places to see what the grace of God can do is to look at what God said to Paul. In 2 Corinthians 12:9 God told Paul: "And He said to me, 'My grace is sufficient for you, for My strength is made perfect in weakness.' Therefore, most gladly I will rather boast in my infirmities, that the power of Christ may rest upon me." Paul suffered great persecution. In fact, it says in verse 7 above this, that a messenger of Satan was sent to buffet him.

This messenger of Satan produced great persecution wherever Paul went to preach the good news about Jesus. Paul asked the Lord three times for the messenger of Satan to be removed from his life. After God informed Paul that His grace was sufficient, Paul went on to preach the good news all around the known world. Paul kept going and he kept winning people to Jesus. How did he keep going and having great success? Paul was able to overcome every problem by the grace of God.

We can also have great success by the grace of God. By the grace of God, we can overcome sin and sickness. By the grace of God, we can obtain victory in life to make it through any obstacle. We never have to be defeated or quit. We can make it to the end of our life and say, just like Paul, "I have fought the good fight, I have finished the race, I have kept the faith (2 Timothy 4:7)."

If you are a Christian, please realize the grace of God is available to you right now. Whatever situation you are facing, the grace of God is on standby for you. God's arm is outstretched to you and He is offering His strength for you to overcome any problem in your life.

If you need God's grace right now say this prayer:

Dear Heavenly Father, I thank You for Your grace. I thank You that Your grace is available to me right now. I realize Your grace is sufficient for any problem in this world. Right now, I receive Your grace. Just as I would accept a birthday gift given to me by a friend, I receive Your gift of grace. I thank You that Your grace is sufficient for me just like it was sufficient for Paul. I know I will overcome this _____ (speak out what you need God's grace for) by Your grace. I thank you that I have Your strength, Your wisdom, and Your favor to be the overcomer You have called me to be. In Jesus name I pray, Amen!

Chapter Nine
WE BECOME
NEW CREATIONS

2 Corinthians 5:17
Therefore, if anyone is in Christ, he is a new creation; old things have passed away; behold, all things have become new.

When we call Jesus our Lord, we immediately become a new creation. This may seem like a strange term, but it gives us great insight into what actually happens on the inside of us when we are saved. In an instant we go from being a spiritual being that is separated from God to having a spirit that is connected to God.

Because of sin, our connection to God had been cut off. Before salvation we did not have a connection to God because sin was separating us. Sin is what cuts everyone off from a relationship with God. Jesus took all of our sin upon Himself so now every human on the planet can be reconnected to their Creator. We were destined for eternal punishment, but Jesus took the punishment that we deserved. Because of His sacrificial life anybody can now become a new creation.

This term "new creation" is very fascinating, if we realize we actually become a new species of humans in Christ. Before Jesus came to earth a Christian did not exist. No one on earth had been a Christian until after the crucifixion and resurrection of Jesus. No one on earth even had the opportunity to become a Christian. Now, everyone can choose to become a new creation and to be in Christ. Everyone on earth can now choose to have a relationship with God, be born again, and have their spirit come alive.

Are you seeing why this is the best news that has ever been told to anybody? No one has to be spiritually dead anymore. This is the most amazing news there is and why millions of Christians are telling people all the time about this good news. We get to tell people they can have eternal life with God and how God wants to come live on the inside of them.

When you start to understand these amazing truths, you can understand why millions of Christians have given their entire lives to tell more people about how to become a new creation.

When someone is spiritually dead, and without Christ, they deserve hell. They deserve all the punishment they receive because they have rebelled against God. Choosing their own path instead of the path of God, they have chosen to ignore their Creator instead of acknowledging Him.

In fact, Romans 1:20 says that everyone is without excuse because God can be seen in creation. If anybody honestly looks up at the moon, they can see that it was created. If they look up at the sun, they instinctively know that it was created. If anybody truly stops to look at their hands, feet, eyes and nose, they will have no doubt they were created and did not just happen to show up on earth.

When someone is honest like this, then they can begin to see how they have sinned against their Creator and are in need of a Savior. It is at that point they can call on the name of Jesus and become a new creation.

At the age of 19, I became a new creation. I

had been in a car accident where I saw someone die right in front of me. I started to become very down and depressed. Even though I had been to church, I had never really thought much about God or even really considered that I was a sinner. I had never given much thought to what I am writing in this book at all.

It was at this point I heard a minister preaching the good news of Jesus. In my parents' living room watching Christian television late at night while the rest of my family was in bed, I sat there watching this man, and it all began making sense. God opened my eyes to see Jesus is Lord. I began to see the ugliness of sin and how real God is.

Right there I bowed my knee and called Jesus my Lord. As I got up from there, I knew I had been changed. I knew I was different. I didn't understand much at that point but now I know I had become a new creation in Christ.

I had been changed on the inside and since that day my life has never been the same. My life has been so amazing and full of blessing and miracles, I would have to write another book to tell you all of it. The point I want to make is that when you become a new creation, you will know it.

This is not a "churchy" religious experience. This is something that changes you on the inside and you want to tell everyone. It is something which suddenly fills you with life. It fills you up with God Himself. This is the greatest thing that can happen to any human on this planet.

If you are reading this right now and you are not a new creation in Christ, please make the decision to call on Jesus wherever you may be. He will fill you with His life and your life will never be the same. You will instantly be filled up with God and there is nothing which can ever top that. No experience on this earth can even come close to the experience of becoming a new creation in Christ Jesus!

Chapter Ten
WE ARE ADOPTED
INTO GOD'S FAMILY

Romans 8:15
For you did not receive the spirit of bondage again to fear, but you received the Spirit of adoption by whom we cry out, "Abba, Father."

In the moment before we call on Jesus, we are in the family of Satan. Because of sin we are separated completely from God's family and, if it weren't for Jesus, we would remain separated. Every person has sinned and fallen short of God's glory (Romans 3:23). This separation is only fixed through a relationship with Jesus. Jesus is the bridge between sinful man and a righteous God. When we call on Jesus, we immediately become part of the family of God. We no longer have Satan as our lord.

The word *Abba* was used by children to address his or her father. This word portrays that we can have a close relationship with God now. Before Jesus, the only people who could have a close relationship with God were those He called and talked to directly such as Moses, Abraham, Samuel, Isaiah, and David.

Anybody on earth can now have a close relationship with God through Jesus. This news is so astounding that it amazes me when people reject it. When we are adopted into God's family, we accept a new Lord and from that point forward we can call God our Daddy forever.

Also, worth thinking about here is the term adopted. Many people think adoption is not as meaningful as being born into a family but when someone is adopted, they are specially chosen to be in a family. We were specially chosen by God to be in His family forever!

He wants us to be with Him forever and ever. Isn't that astounding? God chose you and me to be a part of His family. He was looking for someone to adopt and He chose us. This is such good news it makes me want to shout and dance!

Now we can go to Him anytime we want. We can go directly to the Creator of all things anytime we need. We can cry out to our Daddy for help whenever we desire. I like to use the illustration of my kids coming into my office. They don't knock when they come into my office. They walk right in because they know me and trust me. Because they are not afraid of me, they walk right in.

God has given everyone access to go right into the Holy of Holies through Jesus. When Jesus died on the cross the veil which hid the Holy of Holies (the place where only certain priests could enter) was ripped from top to bottom. This means God did the work for us. Jesus finished the work He was sent to do and God opened up His office for all to come in.

We don't have to stand outside in the cold any longer. We don't have to wonder if God will open the door for us. We can come right into God's office, living room, or family room because now we are family. The door to God's house is unlocked and open for anybody who has been washed clean in the blood of Jesus!

Chapter Eleven
WE ARE ACCEPTED
IN THE BELOVED

Ephesians 1:6
To the praise of the glory of His grace, by which He made us accepted in the Beloved.

Have you ever not been accepted? Maybe you were selected last when kids would choose teams in school. I was somewhat athletic and always bigger than most kids, so I was usually quickly chosen. I always felt bad for those who were chosen last. It never seemed fair they were chosen last and made to feel inferior.

Maybe you weren't invited to the big party and when you found out you were sad. Then, the next day at school you had to hear about how great the party was and you felt like you were weird. You wondered why you weren't included like all the other kids.

The good news is everyone on earth is invited to the party of God. Everyone has been chosen to be a part of God's team. Unfortunately, not everyone wants to be on God's team or go to God's party, but they have been invited. No one has to feel left out, be sad or feel excluded any longer. Anybody can choose to be accepted by God because He has made us accepted in the Beloved.

We don't need to be accepted by anyone else when we have been accepted by God. When God says you are accepted, what else matters? When God has said "I love you," and "You are mine forever," what else matters? When we come into Christ, we are His forever. We are loved by Love Himself.

If men reject us, we do not have to fret because God accepts us. God has a place for us in His house forever and ever. He is never going to kick us out or leave us behind. He will always be there for us. Even when we mess up and take a wrong turn, all we have to do is turn around and go back to God's house. Praise the Lord!

God is crying out through me and hundreds of others that all people are now accepted in the

Kingdom of God. The only qualification is that we accept the sacrifice of Jesus as payment for our sin. The amazing thing is we don't have to do any work to get into the Kingdom of God.

It seems logical that God would say, "If you do this and this and this, then you can come into my Kingdom," but He simply wants us to receive the payment that He has already paid for us. It's like someone buying us a mansion with all the luxuries in the best possible place on earth and saying, "All I ask is that you accept these keys to your house. I have paid for it all. It is yours if you want it." We would have to be crazy to reject those keys.

Please don't reject the keys that allow you to go into the Kingdom of God. Please take those keys and receive the payment that has been paid for you. God is asking you right now, "Will you accept the keys to come into My Eternal Kingdom?" If you have still not made a decision to accept what Jesus has done for you, make that decision now. I guarantee that it will be the best decision you ever make.

Chapter Twelve
WE ARE MADE THE RIGHTEOUSNESS OF GOD

2 Corinthians 5:21
For He made Him who knew no sin to be sin for us, that we might become the righteousness of God in Him.

This verse of Scripture is one of the most amazing verses in the entire Bible. If you actually choose to believe this verse it will revolutionize your life. I am always amazed when people don't want to take this verse (and many other verses) at face value. May we not minimize what God has done for us. Instead, may we be grateful and accept that God has made us completely righteous.

Jesus was made sin for us. The only One who had been completely perfect became sin. He had to take all the sin of the world upon Himself. Imagine taking the blame for every sin on earth. Imagine taking the blame for a mass murderer or a serial rapist. Imagine taking the blame for every horrible act that has ever been done. That is what Jesus did for you and for me. This thought alone should humble us to the point of tears.

This word *righteous* means that we have been completely cleansed and have right standing with God. We have been made pure. Instantly we go from a sinner to a saint and from being completely filthy to being completely clean. We don't have stains that still need to be removed. The stains are all washed away by the blood of Jesus.

We now have right standing with God. Before the crucifixion of Christ, we were enemies of God. We had no right to go into the presence of God. We actually deserved death because of our rebellion against God. Now that we are in Christ, we can enter right into His presence. He welcomes us into His throne room any time of the day. Now when we go to God, we don't need to cower in fear of punishment.

The fear of punishment has been done away with for all of those who have accepted the sacrifice of Jesus. The punishment was all laid on Jesus. He took the beating that we deserved. We deserved the nails in our hands and our feet, but He took them in His hands and feet. We deserved the crown of thorns on our head, but He wore it so we didn't have to.

Every punishment we deserved as sinners, He took upon Himself. By doing this He made a way for us to be in God's presence forever. God now sees us in Christ which makes us able to come boldly into the throne room of God.

We could have never done this on our own. We never could have been made right with God through any of our works which means we all would have been put to eternal death. Every human would have had to suffer forever and deservedly so.

This is why we must be so grateful Jesus did this for us and why we must keep telling people the good news that they can have right standing with God for all eternity because of the work of Jesus.

Chapter Thirteen
WE ARE JUSTIFIED

Romans 5:1
Therefore, having been justified by faith, we have peace with God through our Lord Jesus Christ.

When we declare Jesus is Lord, God says to us, "You are justified." The best way to think about this is in the setting of a court of law. Picture a scene where you are standing before God Himself. As you are standing there, God asks you why you don't deserve death for your sin and rebellion against His laws. The only right answer you can give is to say, "Jesus is my Lord. Jesus paid my debt in full."

As soon as you declare that, the gavel comes down and the judgment is pronounced, "You are not guilty. You are fully acquitted forever of all charges against you. You deserve no punishment. You are free to walk freely in the Kingdom of God forever. You are justified." Hallelujah!

The thing many don't realize is that there is punishment due to them for sin against God. This punishment is eternal separation from God and being forever separated from everything good. Imagine never experiencing anything good again. No more time spent playing with our kids or barbecues with the family. No more days of walking in the park or beautiful days at the beach.

Right now, God sends rain upon the righteous and the unrighteous, but this will not happen forever (Matthew 5:45). Very soon what is due to every human will be paid to them. There is nothing that can stop this soon approaching punishment except the blood of Jesus. The blood of Jesus is the only thing that can stop the wrath of God from being poured out on mankind.

This is why we must be washed in the blood of Jesus and why the blood of Jesus is the most powerful thing that exists. Only the blood of Jesus can stop God's punishment from being paid out or save a lost soul. If we filled every building in the world with gold and silver it would still not be enough to save one single soul but the blood of Jesus has enough power to save every single soul on this planet. There is nothing more precious than the blood of Jesus because only His blood can wash every sin away and make a person completely cleansed, righteous, and justified in the sight of God.

In the Old Testament the Jews put the blood of the lamb on their doorposts as the destroyer came through to kill every firstborn child in every household. God told His people to sacrifice a lamb and put its blood around their doors (Exodus 12:7). Without that blood on their doors they would have suffered the same plague as all the Egyptians. It was only because of the blood that the plague was not able to enter into their homes and had to pass over them. This whole event was, of course, a foreshadow of the Lamb of God Who was to come.

Every human on the planet must have the blood of Jesus on their spiritual house if they want to be saved from the wrath of God. Only through Jesus are we saved from the wrath that is coming. There is only one way to obtain salvation from wrath and it is through Jesus. 1 Thessalonians 5:9-10 says, "For God did not appoint us to wrath, but to obtain salvation through our Lord Jesus Christ, who died for us, that whether we wake or sleep, we should live together with Him."

I could go on and on regarding the wonderful things Jesus did for us. This book only gives an introduction to what Jesus has done for us, but I am asking for you to please make the decision to receive Jesus if you still have not. This is the most important decision you will ever make. This is not something to take lightly. Most people spend more time figuring out what they will eat for dinner than where their soul will end up for all eternity.

If you are still not convinced about who Jesus is and what He has done for you, please keep studying. Many people have studied their way right into salvation because they found it is all true. Find out the truth. Don't just think it will all work out in the end somehow. It will not all work out if you are without a Savior.

I leave you with the words of Jesus. Please listen carefully to His words. In John 14:6 Jesus said, "I am the way, the truth, and the life. No one comes to the Father except through Me."

Chapter Fourteen
GROWING UP IN CHRIST

If you have called Jesus your Lord, then it is time to grow. When we are newly born again, we are a new spiritual baby. Just as a natural baby needs food, a spiritual baby also needs food. There are some things you can do to grow up in Christ.

First, get involved in a church that is on fire for Jesus. Make sure they preach the full Word of God and are not ashamed to shout praises to Jesus. As I say in church, a good way to tell if the church is on fire is to go to the pastor and say, "Will you shout praises to Jesus with me right now." If the pastor looks at you strangely, then find another church.

Secondly, tell someone you have made Jesus your Lord. Jesus wants us to be public with our confession of faith and not be ashamed of Him.

Jesus said we need to confess Him before men (Matthew 10:32). We should not be ashamed to be a Christian.

Thirdly, start reading the Bible, because God calls it our spiritual food. Below I have listed many of my favorite verses. These are just a small sampling, but they will get you started in the right direction. Memorize and get to know these verses below and you will immediately begin to grow up in Christ. If you allow these to become a part of you, you won't even recognize yourself in a few years.

Just as our children grow every night and then suddenly we look and say, "How are you that tall already?" you will look back at your old spiritual self before you were a Christian and say, "How did I get this strong in my spirit?" The answer is you fed on spiritual food. You took the proper nutrients to grow up in Christ.

I would like to end this book with a prayer for you:

Dear Heavenly Father, I pray for the one reading this book. I pray You reveal Yourself more and more to them. I pray they see You in reality and truth. I pray they have the strength to stand up for You. I ask that they would have the boldness they need to call upon Jesus in the midst of any persecution surrounding them. May they be filled with revelation knowledge from Your Holy Spirit. May they see the plan You have for their lives. In Jesus name I pray, Amen.

BIBLE VERSES TO MEMORIZE

James 1:22 But be doers of the word, and not hearers only, deceiving yourselves.

James 4:7 Therefore submit to God. Resist the devil and he will flee from you.

Acts 1:8 But you shall receive power when the Holy Spirit has come upon you; and you shall be witnesses to Me in Jerusalem, and in all Judea and Samaria, and to the end of the earth.

Acts 10:38 How God anointed Jesus of Nazareth with the Holy Spirit and with power, who went about doing good and healing all who were oppressed by the devil, for God was with Him.

1 John 1:9 If we confess our sins, He is faithful and just to forgive us our sins and to cleanse us from all unrighteousness.

1 John 4:4 You are of God, little children, and have overcome them, because He who is in you is greater than he who is in the world.

1 John 4:18 There is no fear in love; but perfect love casts out fear, because fear involves

torment. But he who fears has not been made perfect in love.

Matthew 6:33 But seek first the kingdom of God and His righteousness, and all these things shall be added to you.

Matthew 8:17 That it might be fulfilled which was spoken by Isaiah the prophet, saying: "He Himself took our infirmities and bore our sicknesses."

Mark 9:23 Jesus said to him, "If you can believe, all things are possible to him who believes."

Luke 10:19 Behold, I give you the authority to trample on serpents and scorpions, and over all the power of the enemy, and nothing shall by any means hurt you.

John 3:16 For God so loved the world that He gave His only begotten Son, that whoever believes in Him should not perish but have everlasting life.

John 10:10 The thief does not come except to steal, and to kill, and to destroy. I have come that they may have life, and that they may have it more abundantly.

John 14:27 Peace I leave with you, My peace I give to you; not as the world gives do I give to you. Let not your heart be troubled, neither let it be afraid.

Joshua 1:8 This Book of the Law shall not depart from your mouth, but you shall meditate in it day and night, that you may observe to do according to all that is written in it. For then you will make your way prosperous, and then you will have good success.

Romans 5:17 For if by the one man's offense death reigned through the one, much more those who receive abundance of grace and of the gift of righteousness will reign in life through the One, Jesus Christ.

Romans 6:23 For the wages of sin is death, but the gift of God is eternal life in Christ Jesus our Lord.

Romans 8:2 For the law of the Spirit of life in Christ Jesus has made me free from the law of sin and death.

Romans 8:32 He who did not spare His own Son, but delivered Him up for us all, how shall He not with Him also freely give us all things?

Romans 10:9 If you declare with your mouth, "Jesus is Lord," and believe in your heart that God raised him from the dead, you will be saved

Romans 12:2 And do not be conformed to this world, but be transformed by the renewing of your mind, that you may prove what is that good and acceptable and perfect will of God.

Hebrews 11:1 Now faith is the substance of things hoped for, the evidence of things not seen.

Hebrews 13:8 Jesus Christ is the same yesterday, today, and forever.

Psalm 23:4 Yea, though I walk through the valley of the shadow of death, I will fear no evil; for You are with me; Your rod and Your staff, they comfort me.

Psalm 23:5 You prepare a table before me in the presence of my enemies; You anoint my head with oil; my cup runs over.

Psalm 34:19 Many are the afflictions of the righteous, But the Lord delivers him out of them all.

Psalm 91:7 A thousand may fall at your side, and ten thousand at your right hand; but it shall not come near you.

Psalm 103:3 Who forgives all your iniquities, who heals all your diseases.

Galatians 2:20 I have been crucified with Christ; it is no longer I who live, but Christ lives in me; and the life which I now live in the flesh I live by faith in the Son of God, who loved me and gave Himself for me.

Ephesians 3:20 Now to Him who is able to do exceedingly abundantly above all that we ask or think, according to the power that works in us,

Ephesians 4:29 Let no corrupt word proceed out of your mouth, but what is good for necessary edification, that it may impart grace to the hearers.

Ephesians 4:32 And be kind to one another, tenderhearted, forgiving one another, even as God in Christ forgave you.

Ephesians 6:16 above all, taking the shield of faith with which you will be able to quench all the fiery darts of the wicked one.

Philippians 4:6 Be anxious for nothing, but in everything by prayer and supplication, with thanksgiving, let your requests be made known to God;

Colossians 1:13 Who hath delivered us from the power of darkness, and hath translated us into the kingdom of his dear Son:

1 Timothy 6:6 Now godliness with contentment is great gain.

2 Timothy 1:7 For God has not given us a spirit of fear, but of power and of love and of a sound mind.

1 Thessalonians 4:16 For the Lord Himself will descend from heaven with a shout, with the voice of an archangel, and with the trumpet of God. And the dead in Christ will rise first.

2 Thessalonians 1:3 We are bound to thank God always for you, brethren, as it is fitting, because your faith grows exceedingly, and the love of every one of you all abounds toward each other.

1 Corinthians 2:9 But as it is written: "Eye has not seen, nor ear heard, Nor have entered into the heart of man, The things which God has prepared for those who love Him."

1 Corinthians 9:24 Do you not know that

those who run in a race all run, but one receives the prize? Run in such a way that you may obtain it.

1 Corinthians 13:4 Love is patient, love is kind. It does not envy, it does not boast, it is not proud.

2 Corinthians 4:4 Whose minds the god of this age has blinded, who do not believe, lest the light of the gospel of the glory of Christ, who is the image of God, should shine on them.

2 Corinthians 4:18 While we do not look at the things which are seen, but at the things which are not seen. For the things which are seen are temporary, but the things which are not seen are eternal.

2 Corinthians 5:7 For we walk by faith, not by sight.

2 Corinthians 5:17 Therefore, if anyone is in Christ, he is a new creation; old things have passed away; behold, all things have become new.

2 Corinthians 5:21 For He made Him who knew no sin to be sin for us, that we might become the righteousness of God in Him.

1 Peter 5:8 Be sober, be vigilant; because your adversary the devil walks about like a roaring lion, seeking whom he may devour.

2 Peter 3:9 The Lord is not slack concerning His promise, as some count slackness, but is longsuffering toward us, not willing that any should perish but that all should come to repentance.

Revelation 3:20 Behold, I stand at the door and knock. If anyone hears My voice and opens the door, I will come in to him and dine with him, and he with Me.

Revelation 7:9 After these things I looked, and behold, a great multitude which no one could number, of all nations, tribes, peoples, and tongues, standing before the throne and before the Lamb, clothed with white robes, with palm branches in their hands.

Revelation 21:8 But the cowardly, unbelieving, abominable, murderers, sexually immoral, sorcerers, idolaters, and all liars shall have their part in the lake which burns with fire and brimstone, which is the second death.

About The Author

Vern Frank II is the senior pastor at Pacific Bible Church in Ilwaco, WA. He has been serving in ministry for 29 years in many different positions such as youth ministry, children's ministry, music ministry, prayer ministry, helps ministry, and pastoral ministry.

He and Kaaryn have been married for 27 years; they have three children and they all currently work together to tell everyone they can about the Good News of Jesus.

Pacific
Bible Church

501 First Ave N
PO Box 868
Ilwaco, WA 98624

Pacbible.org

Facebook.com/pacificbiblechurch
Instagram.com/pacificbiblechurch
Youtube.com/pacificbiblechurch